Telling us "these are not / the best of times / to be falling asleep" and arriving just when we need it, Claudia Putnam's *The Land of Stone and River* is cinematic in scope, from its opening haiku—the pebble that pulls down the avalanche—to long, incantatory pieces as tenderly raw as wind-torn wires, reminding us that "we are electromagnetic / beings, animated just as Shelley / knew, drawing lightning to us." ... This is a book of wounds and the wounded, be it the self or society, lost children or cultural traditions, lovers or the land. And yet it is more; it is a book of mending, of healing, and of redemption. Seeded with heavenly bolts of feminist power, of the creator mother, this is a book of love, and this is a book that will be loved.

—Matt W. Miller, author of *Tender the River*
and *The Wounded for the Water*

The Land of Stone and River, by Claudia Putnam, is a riveting book about wild creatures and the personal wilderness of love and loss in a complicated world. Whether she's writing about a lynx in Colorado, a teenage girl shot at the border to Nepal, or her own lost baby, the poems are fierce, honest, moving and yes—often hopeful, too. "Find the tingle," she tells the reader, "the race of life / still there."

—Susan Terris, author of *Familiar Tense*

As raw and powerful as a great wind, Claudia Putnam's *The Land of Stone and River* is like finally getting to step into the sunlight after having been cooped up far too long. ... In Putnam's hands, nature is not that distant, separate entity to be gazed at from the walled-off space of the library or drawing room. Nature is in us and around us and of us, and we are of it. From a woman catching a falling eagle and holding it through its death to another woman believing elk are rearing her aborted daughter, *The Land of Stone and River* is an astonishing, bright presence, that simultaneous slap of wind and burst of sun that affirms "No break / really heals," even as it bestows "peace on all who mourn."

—Melissa Studdard, author of *I Ate the Cosmos for Breakfast* and *Dear Selection Committee*

The Land

of Stone

and River

Claudia Putnam

MOON CITY PRESS
Department of English
Missouri State University
901 South National Avenue
Springfield, Missouri 65897

No part of this book may be reproduced in any form or by any electronic or mechanical means, including information storage and retrieval systems, without permission in writing from the publisher, except in the case of short passages quoted in reviews.

First Edition
Copyright © 2022 by Claudia Putnam
All rights reserved.
Published by Moon City Press, Springfield, Missouri, USA, in 2022.

Library of Congress Cataloging-in-Publication Data

Putnam, Claudia.
The land of stone and river: poems / Claudia Putnam.

2022933094

Further Library of Congress information is available upon request.

ISBN-10: 0-913785-63-6
ISBN-13: 978-0-913785-63-8

Cover art: by Nancy Martin: *New Land IV*, watermedia painting, 29 by 22 inches, 2021.

Text edited by and copyedited by Karen Craigo.
Cover designed by Shen Hsieh.
Interior designed by Michael Czyzniejewski.

Manufactured in the United States of America.

www.moon-city-press.com

TABLE OF CONTENTS

Namgyal Tsering and his family,
wherever they may be

My son, Julian Putnam, and his
brother, Jacob, who I know still
guides us both

The Land
of Stone
and River

Twenty Mountains

HOARD

Sure sign of the end:
This flashlit shining mound: pennies
packrat-piled beneath the shed

Elegy for Snow

And in the winter, which was confined by statute to two months, the snow lay evenly, three feet thick, but never turned to slush.

—*T.H. White,* The Once and Future King

In the time when winter was winter—
I am trying to tell you about it now:
snow, and silence, the way they fell
and then lay, not evenly as in
King Arthur's day, but bunched
like feathers in a comforter.
You know nothing of quilts, either.
Nor can you know of that quiet,
related somehow to cold
and to particular greens of evergreens,
especially to chickadees
who used to perch there, rotund
with secrets of winter.
Now kept by no one.

THIS ISN'T REALLY HAPPENING

My black bird was bigger,
                    my mountains were burning.
          The snows stopped coming

sometime around 1999. The wells
                    dried. The shower sputtering
          with soap in my hair

so I was always late. That tame crow
                    someone set loose spying
          through the skylight, jeering.

How many ways is that? Each year
                    the river runs thinner,
          fleeing its shrinking glacier.

The Arapaho said the thunderbird,
                    black as any bird gets,
          lived just west of here.

Someone must have seen it,
                    the day it flapped away.
          We don't get regular afternoon

stunners the way we used to.
                    You could set your heart on
          those 2 p.m. monsoons. Biblical

lightning, all that water. Now: rusting
                    ponderosas, centuries old,
            disrobing. All good things

must end. Perhaps nightmares
                    also end. Not perhaps
            in our lifetimes.

Poor lost crow, these are not
                    the best of times
            to be falling asleep.

BLACK BIRD

It's not often you see a crow
this low in our canyon.

Maybe he liked flying in and out of the light
while his comrades flapped along the ridgetops.

Mornings, he would strut along our flat roof,
pecking at the skylight, peering in with the late sun.

He was willing to alight on a shoulder or an arm.
The heads of passing drivers would turn.

Many dislike or are terrified of crows
for their history of feeding on the dead.

Our neighbor gardened stooped over,
the black crow pacing her back.

FLUSHED

Running the Highline,
a fleeting thought
of the threat of lions,

turn my head to find
the dogs chasing one.
tail stretched out long,

a comet through my heart.

It ran; the dogs were safe,
just this painful weight
of coincidence

to bear back down
the mountain.
The thought and then

the conjured beast,
the liquid leap
to the tree and then

the long run down,

all those years
running through woods,
sensing but not seeing.

BLUR

Your father coming
home late—a cougar
vaulted the road,
blazed up the driveway.

He floored it,
but the lion outran
his high beams, vanished
on the hillside.

Of course I thought of you.
Who sprang
fully formed into our lives
and died.

WAYS OF THE LION

1.
In twenty snowy mountains
the only thing that lay still
was the lion.

2.
A branch moved,
but it was only snow
sliding.

3.
Another branch moved,
but it was just
more snow sliding.

4.
The woman on snowshoes
only once glimpsed it,
the tail slicing
the corner of her eye.

5.
If you feel watched,
you probably are.

6.
Its scream,
a horse falling through space,
the screech of brakes,

and glass breaking,
is worse
if you hear it at night.

7.
They say to make yourself
large and loud.

8.
Carry a big stick.

9. & 10.
Don't make eye contact.
Don't look away, either.

11.
There's a stench, a zoo-animal smell,
as if the twenty mountains are its cage.

12.
It doesn't care if you're an environmentalist.

13.
For a while she carried mace,
but she didn't feel
any safer.

HEADLINE: MOTHERS GIVEN BACK BABIES
THEY THOUGHT DEAD

20 years I've dreamed of this   the call comes
      they've found him

in a hospital basement on

                      dusty
      life support

just misplaced

                      all these years

he's still doomed

some things you can't change   not even
      in your dreams

But now in Romania

          fairytale

land of ambiguous   endings

dead babies
        given back

Unawake

For the funeral she regrets not having a religion they were too young he was too young for anyone to help them without religion there were pies casseroles but no funeral if it is odd to have a dead kid without a funeral believe it or not that is one thing in America with family thousands of miles away that can fall through the cracks camel a mother's back and there is no heaven. No one else to know him no strength for the parents to speak no priest or preacher to read out some standard lines the mortuary put him in a Styrofoam box and she does not regret not having coffin for the oven. How long does it take for the soul to leave did he need more time before the fire what are wakes for if I should die wasn't that why people sat vigil later she read about DMT research how it might take days for the soul molecule to settle they should have waited funerals kill time so the soul can exit almost any religion would have taught her that much to let him rest let him souffle till he left of his own accord may he rest in peace may she go in peace oh

peace   on all beings peace   on the infant

peace on all who mourn

GOATS

Last night, reading Jane Kenyon,
I dwelled upon selves
within me, living without me.

Goats trail her neighbor to the mailbox.
I've always wanted them, birthings,
homemade cheeses, earthy essays
I'd harvest. Last night, you said

your new wife carries a child,
to be born in the same month
as our own little boy, who died.

Last night, I dreamt of fluffy kids
quieting in my arms, the long ears
tickling my nose and chin. Myself a strong,
straight-backed woman.

LYNX

I saw you floating through snow
light as the snowshoe hare
who in terror leapt before you.

I miss that snow and the winds
it came in on. The work it made:
hungering woodstove,

drifted-in drive, daily ski
from my door to your mountain.
Storm blue of the spruce.

They said you were extinct then,
not yet reintroduced.
I saw you; you looked straight at me.

FIVE DEER

1. *Outside my studio*

Small, bleached skull plate,
short, double-pronged antlers
stripped white. Brown scum

of brain. Waiting for crows
to pick it clean, I prop it
upon a rock. Next day,

found flung

        into a meadow

                my ex-husband owns.

2. *Heartshot*

A stag kneels
outside my bedroom
window.

It's redundant
to put this in a poem;
it *is* a poem:

the bowshot hart
expiring,
lilac-shrouded

bower. Eventually
the hunters come,
exalting.

3. *First date*

Trail run, misting
rain   heightened
color: *silver* pines,
gold leaf, then

crimson beneath
our feet   follow
that trail   ribs
scoured like

an ice cream
tub   intestines
roped upon
the shrubs   sweet

unspoiled head
pools of blood
so bright
in this light

4. *Running late*

Deer along here
so used to cars.
But one outpaces

my brake, cartwheels
to the roadside.
At lunch I return,

track her,
with a neighbor
and a gun.

When she runs,
we know she wants
to live. I still see her,

sometimes, staggering,
having eluded
the lions so far.

5. *New love*

Scarred-heart widowed lover

unpacking from the trunk

of his suicided

sister: two long

antlers, two prongs each, gray

and smooth. I lay them

across my desk, with something like

gratitude

for the crows.

BONE LAMENT (A FAILED SESTINA)

The year my ankle broke
the astrologer warned it was likely
to happen. Skin would rupture,
bones would shatter, plans
would come to naught. Saturn opposite
my sun. This could last for years.

Bone and soul forged together,
broke together. How could it
have happened? The sun hid
while we skied new snow.
Just a twist, a snap heard
before I hit the ground.

Somewhere, on some secret ground,
someone else is wondering
why this is happening. Years go by,
no morphine, just broken bones,
solitary holes, alone,
no hope of healing.

The paramedics made me rate my pain.
Ten the worst that's happened
in years. Labor? As bad as labor?
I thought it might be worse.
My pain threshold lower
than it used to be.

Fentanyl, more fentanyl, no raising
that threshold. Only morphine helped—
I'd taken no morphine, or anything, for labor.
Astrology wasn't helpful there, either,
my son weighted with all those planets
in Capricorn.

While I healed I lay alone
in a bedroom painted the color
of the Puget Sound, where my son was living
on the threshold between college
and life. He uses pot like morphine
and lies like a Capricorn.

I don't know if he'll ever heal,
or stop lying, or why his soul
craves morphine. What ruptured
in him, or exactly when, if I
tortured him somehow, or was it
just some strange twist.

Probably the relatives of detainees
go on living, crying softly
at times, wondering how this could be
happening, trying not to think of the broken
bones and torn souls
which might not ever heal.

I was lucky. While others
were stuck with their stars,
my time alone in that sea-hued
womb was a threshold I crossed,
the morphine shrinking the pain
to the break itself.

Where it burned, a half-dollar or so,
a coin of agony covering the fracture
like a dead eye. We turn dead eyes
to so many lying solitary. No break
really heals. We try to go on
with our plans.

FLEDGES

That was the year fledges dropped
                              like peaches

The dog killed one

The lawnmower another

That was the year of the seventy-two-hour hold

That was the year your stepmother
           was pregnant   and you ran away

              your note said

to drown yourself
        in a deep mountain lake

You said   My body will never be found

           You said   Don't look for me

        Oh birdie

        Oh child for whom we circled and called

These torn nests

how alike to one another they all appear

when the birds are gone

in fall

CAIRN STONE

This is the rock he lifted
to lay upon a cairn
in a high place.

This rock, warmed by the near sun,
felt right, somehow, in his hand.

He decided to carry it down
to his mother, who lay in bed,
recovering.

It is so easy to please
a mother. Just to think of her
for a moment, from a high place,
and to carry that thought to her

in the form of a stone.

SHE WHO WAS ABLE TO EMBRACE THE EAGLE KNEW ITS LAST THOUGHT

An eagle is no blackbird.
It was dying when she crested the pass
And came upon it, lurching
For the sky, hovering at eye level.
She pulled her car over.
The wings five feet, stretching, outstretching,
The bird falling, falling.

She went to the eagle, arms wide.
She caught it on the fourth
Fall. At first it forced her arms
Apart. But the second time she caught it,
It folded its wings.
After a few moments it died.

She said she felt a heaviness greater than
The eagle's weight. A grief
Over leaving the sky and dying on earth.
A sadness blanketing twenty mountains.
What do you do with that gift, standing there
Clutching the corpse of an eagle?

The Land of Stone and River

SASQUATCH

Everyone believes in Sasquatch
Tell me you don't, inside
or at least hope
there's something big out there
still unidentified
secret, wild

AFTER FLOWERS

(For a girl shot by Chinese border guards while crossing from Tibet to Nepal, Sept 30, 2006. Witnessed, videotaped, YouTubed.)

How we love to name our daughters
after flowers.

Kelsang, lavender shade of the seventh
chakra, so close to heaven—
thriving like the edelweiss
in the high air, sipping on the snows.

Is the daughter named
       for the holy lama,
       the flower for the lama,
       or the lama for the sweetness,
in the purple flower?

She is seventeen. Is it loveliness
we wish for our daughters
when we name them after flowers?

Delicacy? Daintiness? An efflorescence?
Daisy. Lily. Iris. Violet. Rose.

We must know, when we name our daughters,
   how fleeting is their beauty, how soon
they will fall, how quickly
   the hard seasons will come upon them.

Kelsang Namsto, you fell
    in the high snows and were left there
    by those who had to go

into their own, later autumns. We saw you snapped
from the stalk, we saw you bleed into the headwaters.

You were seventeen.
We saw you go.

As the Wind Comes Among Us

1. Great Sand Dunes National Park, Colorado

In the right light, they could be hills,
green with ricegrass, a scatter of willows,
as refugees driven from the plain, from
other mountains, they yield to what
brought them here.

They are only resting

in the shadow
of the Sangre de Cristos.

2. Entrada IV: Tailings

Stirred with metal, the dunes
sift, shrug, shoulder the range.
Where the wind found gold
in the sere San Luis Valley, I have
no idea. From afar, the San Juan
Mountains? Such gold as the miners
missed, waiting for the wind to find,
then laid down as gilt

in hollows,
along ridgelines.

3. Entrada III: Conquistadores

Sangre de Cristos.   Conquistadores
named everything for Christ's body—

late afternoon illuminates this valley
with the rose of sacrifice,
the sierra, the very air,
reliquary,
blood mist.

It is the name of the range
these five hundred years,
though the mountains are young,
have eons yet to go.

4. Entrada VI: Karma Thegsum Tashi Gomang

Into this red valley
come the monks, come
the nuns, refugees
from another conquered land
older than God.

Depositing relics
      wood from the bodhi tree
      water from a cave
      where a Buddha prayed
      mementos from each
      of the Karmapa's sixteen
      previous lives
in their repository,
a shrine uplifted

against Kit Carson Peak,
north of the roving dunes.

This wind, it moves
in circles, does
it not.

These relics, this reliquary,
blessed by the Karmapa in his
sixteenth lifetime, who will again
visit in his seventeenth lifetime,
this valley, itself a vessel
of Christ's Blood, the white peaks
beaming above the red air,
haunting the valley floor as if
taunting little men who cannot
look above what they are looking for.

As here,
as now,
as the wind
drops the sand, the gold,
combs through the sangre-red peaks,
before dirtying itself,
again,
with Kansas topsoil,

a sign at the American shrine says anyone
touched by the wind that touches the shrine
is liberated.
Let us stand downwind.

The sign says there are 84,000 paths

to enlightenment. May all refugees

find one.

5. Lament for one refugee, my housecleaner, Namgyal
Tsering, taken by night from his cell by ICE officials
while awaiting a deportation hearing scheduled for the
following day, and placed on a plane to Nepal

Namgyal went walking
he had no shoelaces

Homeland Security
took them and his jacket

They disallowed
any money for the bribes

In LAX he borrowed a cell phone
so we'd know where

At last we heard
he endured the interrogation

in Kathmandu and walked
to India and we're not sure where

Years before he'd walked
into the wind
in sneakers just as they say

over the Himalaya
from Tibet to Kathmandu
then come to America

Homeland Security
sent him walking again

So somewhere Namgyal
we hope
wears Tara's cloak on his shoulders

Parents in Tibet a wife in India
a son in America the lost laces
binding all of us

His sneakers flapping
along those paths

Those paths those people
walk along

6. (Namgyal & the Karmapa)

With Namgyal aflutter
in her womb, his mother
climbed those mountains, which are

the most far, the most high
and which so many of her
people had already climbed,

past the guns of the border,
seeking the blessing
of the Karmapa

on her unborn child, before
reversing her journey,
her husband beside her,

over that nineteen
thousand foot pass, to their
bereft village in plundered

Tibet. Sometimes, not often
enough, I try to
imagine those gales.

> *Karma Thegsum Tashi Gomang is a Tibetan Buddhist retreat center and community founded in Crestone, Colorado, by the sixteenth Karmapa. The Karmapa, a tulku from a lineage older than the Dalai Lama's, is currently in his seventeenth incarnation. Namgyal's name was bestowed upon him in utero by version sixteen. Adequate but necessarily incomplete accounts of Namgyal Tsering's "removal" by Immigration and Customs Enforcement [ICE] were given in the Denver and Boulder newspapers in June 2008, for example, www.dailycamera.com/ci_13098301.*

7. Entrada I: Crestone Conglomerate & the Aquifer

(Found compilation)

> *I will spend the rest of my life*
> *going after that water.*
> *—Texas Commissioner, the Lower Rio Grande Compact*

In the land of stone and river, godless,
known by wind, that is, the continent
we name Gondwana, near the place we call
Equator, the range we term Ancestral

Rockies rises,

groundwater seeping beneath its flanks, mixing—
is this memory—minerals to
iron oxide, turning in Time
to hematite—desire, surely—
rosy on the range we christen

bloody in our Time, still the Time
of the Conquistadores, and
it is dizzying,

& it is dizzying!
to see how many things have to happen
to explain what has to happen to
explain what is in the color of this rock

Crestone Conglomerate emerges
from several rock cycles
sedimentary basins tilted
into massifs recycled into
new troughs, precipitated,
cemented into more hardrock.

That's three rock cycles
you're looking at.

You begin to get
           kind of
           dizzy
           as you realize

how many
        things had to
        happen to explain
        what's in
        this rock.

Thousands
of feet
of sand
and gravel
groundwater
flowing slowly
through the
bottom gravels
precipitates
dissolved
chemicals
cements
any rock
at the bottom
like concrete
cements it
like concrete.

Crestone Conglomerate is unique as it
does not break as other conglomerates
do and all four fourteeners Kit Carson
Crestone Needle Humboldt Peak and
Crestone itself together form a single
solid outcrop of amalgamated stones

& these huge conglomerate boulders have been

sitting on the glacial outwash
thumbing their noses

at erosion

& the range knifes
the valley from the Plains,
from Music Pass with the wind,
having dropped its dust,
chording the cliffs with song,
you look across Colorado to Kansas.

Mountains of the White Light,
they are said to have once been
called, by people not pale,
the snowpack sending

millions of acre-feet
in surface water, wind-ruffled, landed on
by migrating geese and cranes, lacing

through the valley each year.
Some percolate to ancient waters
             enclosed
in rock and clay
thirty thousand feet down.

Deeper than you think, someone else says.
No one knows how deep.

Thousands of feet of sand, groundwater

dissolves chemicals   precipitates   cements the rock
like concrete, basins uplifted into mountains,

godless,
each rock cycle.

—USGS Circular 1349: The Geologic Story of Colorado's Sangre de
Cristo Range, *David A. Lindsey*
—*"Rock of Ages,"* interview with Geologist Jim McAlpin, PhD, in the
Crestone Eagle
—San Luis Aquifers, *James Aber, Emporia State University*

8. Entrada IV: Rio Grande del Norte

Come

the tenders, growers, herders,
hearts deep as the aquifer
that turns the sand to earth and
green. Though wind pummels the ears,
though dirt may fill the eyes, they follow
the river north

from lands layered in conquest, souls
hanging deep. In the evening a sudden
coolness. What gold is in the air

shows itself.

Dusk bathes them
in the sangre de Cristo.

9. Entrada II: The Old Ones

The last earthquake jumped this plane
four feet. Hot springs pump
lithium from the faultline. Wind
builds dunes from the old
sea floor, where the aquifer steeps,
a promise and a memory.

This valley so broad and long
it could swallow Israel
and still look young.

And there's a shadow
in the basin, a crater,
and it is said:

> Long ago, a sipapu
> opened into this valley,
> as a navel, so Pueblo
> and one day Navajo peoples
> could climb into this layer,
> from the last underworld—

AFTER AFRICA

It doesn't start with Earth,
but let's start with the earth   It doesn't
start with the Americas but let's
start with the Americas
After Africa the sea triumphant
After Africa continental diaspora

After Gondwana
After Africa   Sliding north
after Antarctica
with rain washing Appalachia
to the seas, inland and outland
with Cascadia afire
Rockies on the rise
          for the third time
After dinosaurs (except herons, condors)
heartlands sublimated in water
salt, fresh, shallow, in some places
deeper, swallowed beneath capstones
and Nevada in various stages of appearance
          and dis-

Do stones remember other fires, other selves
          sleeping in their beds? What can the rivers
          recall of rains from other skies? Glaciers
          blushing with sand from deserts far, blanching
          with ash from distant volcanoes

Swift winds tell swift tales that swiftly fade

News of other lands unreliable   Birdseed
Blown-out cloud   Ash   Whisper of China
Africa a memory, Europe
            a secret

After Africa   primate diaspora
footprints in dust red handprints left
some never recorded

Pause here   doldrums   unruffled water
above a chasm   Atlantic   Appalachian
Cascadian   Antarctic

African

What you know is that these
are not the names

Tamarin capuchin howler
ancestors wrangling their logs
across that old, smaller ocean—
the first invasion
the first
entrada

until Beringia
and the outriggers from Polynesia?

Awaiting the Olmec, Toltec, Maya
to be created, gods?

Those hearts, those bodies bloodying
the pyramid stair
whose hearts
hearts for whom?

The Americas collided
their place of joining
long container,
such a terror
such a terrible place waiting
And:

towers to keep the sun
in the sky—no, too simple:
to keep an age
alive—children tortured
drowned
to please the rain
to please the rain
to fill the rivers
parents (proudly? it is said) in attendance
to fill the lakes
(dried, dying now, it must be said)
and rivers

in the land of stone and river
godless all those years before
In the land of stone
of river
where water had flowed for
millions of years
before primates

sailed or walked
where sun had always shone

Did rivers ask for this:
now you've entered
please drown your children

Do they still?

(Was it the *stone* that demanded Isaac?)

5-Earthquake 5-Earthquake
this fifth age of the land
will end in rupture
without hearts to feed
the sun

The land speaks, does it not   Its
fossils speak you dream them
Feathered serpents dragon lords
Thunderbirds and water monsters
Quetzalcoatl   O dinosaur   The land speaks
to those who hear, but does it listen?

These gods so late to the continent
Fierce ones, beings of fierceness
inhuman ones, souls
unalike to humans   having never

created people in their
own likenesses
Said spirit of rock
to spirit of rain

on a day when sun warmed limestone
dappled through eddies
What are these animals
lips and eyes resin-sealed   floating
in our waters?

They are children said sun   What are children said rock
It cannot be explained said rain

The prior ages, it is said
beasts, storm, fire, floods were
their ends   Isn't that right
didn't the world end that way
over and again
dinosaurs and sabertooths
hurricanes   volcanoes
seas intruding   receding
didn't the land of stone and river
come to many terrible ends?

After Africa   after the primate diaspora
5-Earthquake   And doesn't the ground
shake?

TRAJECTORIES

The Oregon Trail is marked in places
by wagon ruts and vegetation
in clumps thicker and greener,
though invisible to the naked eye.
With infrared, could you trace
the trail from grave to grave?

When we built the new house, I left
our infant son beneath the lilac
in the old yard. Who owns that home
now owns his bones.

Those children left behind—

while the husks of their mothers
move on, and on, one foot,
one foot before the other,
newborns beneath cornerstones
of new lives, and Isaac, whose name
was mirth, bound to the well-worn stone,

knowing, as mothers know, that God
destroyeth the hope of man,
hope and mirth bound over
for the promised land.

VEDAUWOO

Go down the way you came,
said the rock.

Your clamps, bolts, shouts,
laughter, your triumph

have no place
upon this rock
upon this rock
there is no place

for laughter, for crowing
for your bottled water.
Upon this rock,
those who came
before lay with empty
stomachs, waterless,
crying dry-eyed for
visitations. Anyone
with eyes to see can
see this was a place
where sometimes spirits
sent seekers back,
hair gone white. Come
not to play. Come not

unprepared, unversed,
unfasted, undanced, with
no eyes or ears. Millennia,
generations, mammoths,

horses, camels gone
to their deaths before
spirit, human understood
one another.

This unwritten, unmade land,
which God never knew,
where Jesus never walked.

Go back down the way you came.

READING OCTAVIO PAZ

Midnight
              between
Mexico City and the highlands
the night
                        spun
              into deep velvet
air so dense I couldn't understand
how we could pass—

along the way the fabric
                        punctured
by lorries of soldiers
                                        dead set
in armor, ceremonial guns bristling

              obsidian swords

              helmeted, alert,
laid by in rest areas. We were
              afraid
                        to take our ease
for seven hours.

We had the windows rolled
down, thick tropical air flowing
in, a weave reaching back
                                        or down
or covering or connecting
so that I could hear us,

ourselves, talking quietly
in the car as it traveled
its curving line along
      the highway past
            lakes dying of lilies,
  of human
        interference
into the lop-topped mountains
murmuring with
our words   of today,
English   and   Spanish,
the driver trying to teach me
while trying to learn, each of
us folding into the other's
      head some small way.

Talking of soldiers, pitched
against la violencia, still no
stopping for the restroom,
in Mexico
    for centuries
    no rest,
    only un-,
as well as any narco, they
could raid an americana,
blame it on a driver.

The night
        so dark, so velvet,
     so thick with oxygen

                              exhaled from plants.
It let us through. The soldiers
couldn't see us,

                              I thought,
I thought maybe we weren't
on the same highway as
the soldiers.
                    Do you hear
that?

The driver, surprised:
          It happens sometimes,
not often.

Cascade of voices, riding the
fabric, this magic
              carpet, flow of
syllables,
history of words,
languages.
                    As if we were
driving not through black
and empty
night but past
markets and carnivals, busy
populations.

On one curve
          louder, another
silenced.

Reaching el Lago del
Pátzcuaro, where the lake,
still huge, though

            a fragment

       of itself in the
time of empire,
still fights
its lilies to live, where
the old temple hulks
beneath the cathedral,

               beneath
               the entire town—
          where the empire never buckled
      to the Aztec,
      so the bloodlines,
           the lines of blood

straighten.

One day a horseman rode past
in the town, English-erect
          in the Spanish
          saddle.

To see is not
to regard.
To be seen is not
to be regarded.

The horse's fine
fetlocks, its hooves clicking
upon agonizing cobbles.
　　　　Riding it
　　　　was something ancient,
　　　　　something old something cold.
Do not tell me not to judge.

　　　　　　　What happened here,
　　　　　　　in México, was
　　　　　　　never anything good.

What if one day we said:
　　　　Only the Germans may
　　　　speak about or judge the
　　　　Nazis?

Turks, a fine people,
　　　　too bad
　　　　about the Armenians, Kurds.

The Americans, what is it
　　　　with the Americans, fucking
　　　　the whole world.

You, Octavio, stand on your
ancient balconies
　　　　pondering syllables

            incomprehensible
  as crows   spreading   into
            night.

            Inside
    the hollow
    José María Morelos y Pavón
            statue on its island,

    paintings illuminate so many
                    lost words.

A hollow man, a hollow man, standing in a
dying lake, soon to be a desert like the plain,
a hollow man erect on this island
in this gasping lake, this island
with its top flattened, lopped,
like the pyramids whose prayers are lost,
because the gods are lost, this island
with its top lopped like the mountains
surrounding.

The first turning of the stairs,
blood drawn by the first rulers
            remembered, Tzintzuntzan:
            whips, slaves,
second turning of the stairs,
            whips, blood, horses,
            the Conquest,
turning,
            revolution, horses,

blood, guns,
turning, federales, jeeps,
guns
turning, SUVs, guns,
blood, la Familia.

Now that
you stand in the hollow man's fist, upraised,
look out over the lake:

one day in time
fires flared from ruins that were not
ruins, drums boomed across the
water, and then

we cannot be sure what happened.

The murals are memory. Slaves,
blood. St. Gertrudes martyred
in the plaza, blood gushing from her breast,
merry fat babies
lapping

at the fount.

Oh México you drink
as you did before, do not
tell me not to judge.

At the top a hipster—glasses, sideburns—

sprints to catch. You are from America! I
lived in America for two years. Denver,
so beautiful.

Many
          try their English. They
speak our language, descending
that bloody spiral staircase.

In Cortez's palace,
zócalo, Cuidad de México,
a guide told Americans:
See Diego Rivera's crucified
          Christ, feel
the Mixtec confusion,
why worship
a god in so much pain?

And why would they, I say
to my son,
          the Templo Mayor
a few feet away,

          layers of burnt
altars for burnt hearts, built by
          ruler   upon   ruler,
          the people not the gods
          in their agonies.

It is hard said a young man.
On a bus. I didn't write down

exactly what he said.
Something like. We would say
life is hard, but he said in this
life it is hard to get any power.

He was twenty-five, he spoke
English well, he had been to America.
For two years, that is what

they all said, two years in America.
He said come to my house, listen
to my reggae music, when I play

I feel a little power. Had it not been
for the tourist advisories, la violencia,
telling us he was a barbarian,

we would have gone, learned much
more than we did. It is so hard
to get any power.

In this life.

Don't tell me I should wait.
Let the man speak for himself.
I was on the bus with him in Pátzcuaro
with the lilies strangling the lake,
Chinese choking livelihoods from reed weavers,
        copying designs from pottery makers
        copper workers, wood
        artisans and luthiers,

workshops going back
to the days of indigenous empire,
so that now Michoacán

        exports its people.

He told this to me, I want to tell
you what he said.

While he spoke I
thought of my baby
choking to death,
drowning
in his own blood.
There was nothing—

In this life,
it is so hard to get any
power.

One day my son
stood atop a staircase
overlooking the lands of lost
Tzintzuntzan, assuming
it is lost

               (Paz: "lost islands" in
         the evaporated
                  el Lago del México,

and I thought, reading, My lost places,
Lyonesse, Avalon,
are on another continent
and not mine)

assuming Tzintzuntzan
is lost, I don't
know, I'd have to ask,
I do not know
the right people to ask:
Was it ever
lost? The lake, islands, cities,
the flat-topped mountains.
Inside the cathedral, glyphs,
meaning what, speak to
the congregation. Does it
hear?
       Who placed
       those blocks, gathered from
       the old temples, in which
       configurations, decided to
       turn them in which
       directions, was it
       a decision that certain
       glyphs face those who pray
       to the new god?

My son's hair long thick wavy
with rainy-season moisture, he looks
happy in this air, high altitude
yet thick with planted oxygen.

Later in México City in the palace
courtyard there he is his hair
contemporary with sixteenth century
European architecture
looking young as he was
charismatic as he was people stopping
as they did to point: da Vinci! In the
olive groves where bearded long-
haired Jesus lay encased in glass
nuns stared, no doubt the hair
also that gliding water-sliding
way of striding, with some concern.

                Now, he is emptied for
the moment, pale, hunched. I know
why, hate to think of it, lost
in cities of his own country, when,
amid the interstices of the centuries,
he seemed so at home in México.

It is hard, said the young man,
in Pátzcuaro. Define hard, I do
not know how you define it. It
seemed, that moment on the bus,
that we were all on the same bus.

I do not
know what my son was thinking,
that moment, on that bus,
but I could see he was

thinking.
Is a man—Paz—brown-skinned, and
traveling in a brown-skinned land—India—
more empowered to be wrong
than a woman—me—white and traveling
in a brown-skinned land?

My son said: Mom! The reason
everything takes so long here is
you're fixing the roof, first you make
the tile. If you stain the vigas,
you make the stain. Then you sit
with a pounding head for three days.
The man who digs the compost holes
at this Buddhist retreat,
9x9x9 feet, is 80 years old,
weighs 90 pounds, my son said.

Land of problem-
            solving, of people getting
            things done.

            And the ruins sweating,
cowering, lurking, waiting. It is said
of them. Sweating and waiting. Who
knows how many still buried?

                        We don't know.

Archaeologists don't know.
Experts are unsure.

Surely *someone* knows.

Ask enough someones.
                    In the village
of Cobá. Seven centuries of triumph
over that hideous city.

          Seven hundred years
a village.   My village in New
England three hundred years alive.
Still there, hating, guarding.

                    I believe
it takes a village. It takes a child. It
is grueling, a small village. You build
a village, or you build Cobá.

                                             Priests,
pyramids, sacrifice, or the village

square for seven hundred years,
it is the same. It is either/or.

               Atop the pyramid
in the shrine rooms, an atmosphere.

          It is the same all over México, an
altitude, even in the lowlands.
If you did not know what went on
               here you would know what went
               on here. The voices weep with pain and

pride.
The village thought primitive,
          its lost knowledge,
               those bold monuments
bemoaned. Turned from, before
Cortés. Yet the people live.

To be direct I want to know
what's inside or under,
                    mainly inside,
those mountains
around el Lago del Pátzcuaro.

No one knows, I'm told.
They haven't excavated. Someone
knows, I'm sure.

Just this year village dwellers
came to archaeologists, revealed
a cave of Maya artifacts. See?
Someone
knew.

I am only asking
          which came first

mountain

or pyramid

pyramid or mountain

Did they level the tops of those mountains
to match their pyramids? That's some
monumental architecture.

Now Michoacán
exports its people.

It is so hard
to get any power—
            blood, whips, guns, blood.
            It always
            has been

STARFUCKERS

*Often at the after-reading party a visiting poet is surrounded by three co-eds,
starfuckers who expect him to choose a winner.*

—Donald Hall

That co-ed, her agenda,
call it the Eve agenda. Her very own hunger,
curiosity, interviewing the natives, reaching for
low-hanging or higher fruits, no particular order.
The oldest story in the oldest land, so we're told.
The oldest place in which stories were told, we're
told, though that peninsula, a continental bridge,
is a rift, the Red Sea splitting, building new land,
volcanoes vomiting in the time of Moses.

In another ancient land,
"Adirondacks" worn to nubs, "Ancestral
Rockies" turned ass-over at the roots of the new,
a woman went out to lie in the grass, or in
a forest clearing, or in a cleft in some rocks,
or along or in a stream. A ray of the sun or a
beam of the moon found her. We women
know the stir of sunlight on bare skin.
Argent kiss of the stars sliding along arms,
thighs, it raises the hair, the slip of the moon
on the shoulder, the belly. This woman moved
with pleasure, she did, fellows, she moved. With
a pleasure all her own out there alone in the
land of stone and river, that old godless land.

What is born of
moving with pleasure in the rays of the sun or moon,
stars, while lying in grass, on rocks, in water—
the stories would not be stories were there not
consequence, though it does feel, does it not,
as if the tellers, all of them, pause here to spy on
this *movement*, this image of a woman apart
from her tribe, moving with pleasure.

Something doubled or something
halved, twins, usually, havoc-making heroes, or
half-beast/half-man, half-man/half-god. Dangerous
and at the root of all story. In the land of stone and
river, women opened to the lights of heaven. In
those days stars could not resist brave desirous
women lying in grass, in water. They fell to earth,
fucked them. Oh baby.

DRIVING U.S. 50

I remembered the line from the Hindu scripture, the Bhagavad-Gita;
Vishnu is trying to persuade the Prince that he should do his duty and,
to impress him, takes on his multi-armed form and says, "Now I am
become Death, the destroyer of worlds."
   —*Robert J. Oppenheimer, famously, of the first test explosion of an*
   atomic bomb, misquoting Krishna, *who said he had become* Time,
   destroyer of worlds.

Nevada: becoming
another Red Sea
the ocean bottom
already laid only sage
to be cleaned away
when the Time comes
            as it will
            as it always does
            as it has
            & as it will again.

For now range after
mountain range
here mined for weapons
there hollowed
for storage of spent
weapons & yet here
burrowed beneath
for hiding explosions
of weapons.

Giddily down into the basins spying
the next range purple across the next reddened
readying sea floor there is an odd expectant

emptiness.

Clean like shorelines.

& when
blocks that manifest
to our eyes
as mountain ranges
have ripped Nevada
      to pieces
         having folded up
         over themselves
         having stretched
         all the sierras flat
         as all
         the basins

the waters will flood in radioactive.

These drives across Nevada silent:

there is
plenty of Time.

Nervestorm

Liveing's term "nerve-storms" is an incomparable metaphor, for one cannot avoid visualizing the slow gathering of forces and tensions in the nervous system, the sudden breaking of an electrical storm, the ensuing serenity and clear skies.

Migraine and neighboring disorders [epilepsy, manic depression] ... are distinct and individual, but nevertheless have borderlands in which they merge into one another.

—*Oliver Sacks*, Migraine

Awakening

Anything with water is alive
Why does the moon turn up
As dull death when it is a plate an ear
A scythe of light a womb so deep
It took a bomb to stir the seed

POETICS

With appreciation to Carolyn Forché and Robert Bly

The moon swinging on its black cord
assuaging the darkness, the daily papers,
the pistol reclining on its cushion.
Chekhov did warn us about the gun.

You can't blame the beavers in their ponds
or the grass with its perfumes. You can't
blame horses. You can't blame
the dogs barking, or the parrot

on its terrace. You can't blame the wife
with her mangoes and her bearing away
the dishes. You can't blame the poet.
The moon pendulums. It assuages.

Bottles kneecap your enemies, cut hands
to lace. Only themselves to blame.
Poetics demands what poetics demands.
Chekhov warned us about the gun.

MIGRAINE

Late, dusty, leaving   the lonely lane
we rode high   on the red range
seeking someplace   for sound sleeping
for setting up camp   a sign bullet-pierced
warned wayfarers   wandering, to ware:
don't trespass, don't cross   dare not
rile the men riding   rough round here.

We kept on, creeping   cagily along
laughing, looking   leerily around
cattle, cowboys   camping on the crest
of the range. We thought   a rig we'd passed was theirs
a trailer in the trees   a tangle of aspen
a lounging man with liquor   light beer, or lemonade
on the porch, pensive   as we passed.
We stirred cream into Kraft   mac and cheese
                            No one came gunning.

In the southwest   the sky flashed.
Storm or sheet?   We shot our mouths.
Soon the storm   settled it. Our
friends found their tent   We flew
to the car, clamped   into crash restraints.
Such a storm never   seen before
lightning lashing   leaping, curling
unstretching, then whirling   in stripes round itself
making balls, many   to mushroom
like bombs booming at us   babies, huddled in the car.

We thought our friends dead.   They emerged
soaked, ignorant, having   sealed their eyes.
Few have viewed the raw   fire of St. Elmo.
The store of the year unleashed   in that storm that night.
The meadow unmarked as if   made as a stage
for electricity to exercise for less   elevated strikes
on golf courses and goal-directed   gallivanting on cliff sides.

As for supper, we sighed,   started over, abashed.
Floating sleepless in the flimsy   fiberglass tent,
I heard aftershocks of cows   eeyowing with anger
tripping over guywires   trailing across their
favorite meadow after   the frightful storm.
Each time I too jumped.   Try the night
with animals unseen   antagonizing your shelter.

Terrorized for trespassing by   this terrific storm,
we packed, proceeded   over potholes
to the main road, making for   the monument
    of dinosaurs.
No one knows what causes

                        the malady of megrim.
That night on bald   knob-top where cattle knights
succor their souls with   solutions, infusions unknown,
St. Elmo afire   a-raging, aroar,
I was outside one, looking   in, inside
looking out   likewise.

LIMBIC

danger stirs

a chain a spiral
echoes
    in the sub-arachnoid

space or in
the amygdalae

where the wires
    criss

in the medulla
in the pontomedullary
    junction

in the thalamus,
in the hypothalamic pituitary adrenal
axis of evil

in the hypothalamus
where serotonin melatonin
testosterone scramble

they say the lizard is

no longer in
one place lurking
the limbic is

        dispersed
your higher
processes set
with tripwires

danger danger danger
you're not
allowed out
        at
night

NERVESTORM

[Inner?] child writhing
hands on head
neck turning head snapping
this way that
you'd stop it if
you could get close enough
can't/won't
so ugly
ugly ugly child
contorted so
what conturbat
what possesseth
seeming so much larger
than yourself
than someone so
small
seeming legion
we dare not
we do not dare

EARTH SHADOW

The moon has turned its dark face around.
Just a ball of stone, a marble. It could fall;
an invisible wire suspends it.

The moon
has turned its dark face to earth.

The deer move through the trees as if there are
no lions. I am lying out here
as if there are no lions.

Though there are.
And the deer, knowing this,
still move through the trees.

They are deer; they must pass among the trees.
And I must lie upon this chaise,
watching eclipsed rock

that must fall, all lights one light, when we plunge
together to the sun. Look how dim our beacon
has become,

its dark face twisted round.

Titania

Riverton, Wyoming, August 21, 2017

Evening queen,
sought from childhood, never seen.
Night's raiment, whispering web,
rushing to seize her day.

Many sobbed, hid their eyes,
or had them burnt.

      Cool hand upon fever of noon, touch
      of silver, metal of moon and star. Lovely
      now, once crowned, once crowned, violet
      spilling from silver-circled brow.

My heart will
always ring with those strings
played along my spine. Fairy queen,
let us wonder longer. If only
the diamond ring
were a promise.

LAMICTAL: PRELUDE TO THE FIRST DOSE

a modified sestina

Tonight there is no TV, the satellite clotted
with snow. I left on the outdoor light
so I could watch the flakes flowering
the budding lilacs. I am missing
San Francisco, that feeling of the earth shifting.
Though I'm calm, having been alone all week.

You're off in Jackson this week,
evenings at the Million Dollar Cowboy bar, clotted
with tourists. Days in Rendezvous Bowl, shifting
from edge to edge in the flat light
of spring storms. You always miss
mountains, I know, they're where you bloom.

I like the energy of spring light
and the way the lilacs rise up weakly,
laden with snow. Electricity flowers
in me, so we'll use this new drug to clot
that hemorrhage. Who knows what might shift,
if there are pieces of me I'll miss.

You said you'd leave if this kept up, the shifting
moods and rages. I said anger was a light,
all women had anger flowering,
in their souls, red stars, pulmonary clots,
women feel angry week after week,
yearning for the men who are missing.

But tonight I feel calm and bright.
It's because you're away skiing this week.
If no one disturbed me, who knows what might bloom,
what work I might do without drugs, before shifting
again into despair, because I'd miss
you, inevitably. My throat knots

at the thought of you shifting
away from me, switching off the deck light,
going off to sleep in your uncluttered,
quiet way. I hate to close my eyes on a flower,
but you can do it, there'll be a new bloom next week,
you're not afraid of what you might be missing.

I don't want to miss you. The wind has unknotted
the lilacs. What's shifted is I want to be loved.
When the week ends, bring white flowers.

The Battle of Brintellix

in this land winning   a lasting home.
   —*from (last line) "The Battle of Brunanburh,"*
      tr. from the Old English by J.R.R. Tolkien

Nothing should be this easy.
                           —*from "Zoloft" by Maggie Dietz*

Nothing is more noisome   than knowledgeable people
believing themselves to be   best at guiding in grief.
Over that awful summer   I ordered suicide
instructions from the   internet,
favoring bags filled with   floaty helium,
though I also thought   then, of guns,
            a lot.

An island assailed   was I, with
my enemies amassed   no obstacles for them,
my gates down.   No guesses what
            betrayals led to this.
Wielding first what   looked well like logic:
Such a small island   spake they,
so easily overwhelmed   awash in waves,
Why defend it?   Why defy us?
Why keep weaving?   The wear can't
            be repaired.
Abdicate! This island   an heir far
            stronger requires,
your love a truer one.   I lacked for arms.

It happened such   harboring in a nearby
marketplace, gun merchants   mailed flyers

for pistols. Buy pieces   priced cheaply—
buy Berettas and   Bauers, get Colts now.
Bullets stop brains   stop brutalizing voices.
                                        Then I
heard about helium   a helper, gentle,
its exit bags offering   elegant solutions,
less cleanup for   loving husbands
                    and chums.

                              But my
doctor had a drug   just developed, to assist
in the battle, newly branded   "Brintellix"—
brilliance + intelligence—trust   big pharma
                    to come up with that.
Peeved, I thought it   pointless, what good
could come of such chicanery?   Courage! he said.
                    Not a wimp-out! A weapon!

My star-flame I should   say I drew,
my sleep-monsters I fought.   In sooth,
it made me seasick.   I managed barely
                    to stand.
No halo lit my hair.   No harp sounded.
No raging demons routed   or retreated even.
No dragons expired.
                              Only I did not die.
After days enough not   dying, I lived,

though lurking beyond   limning waves,
shadowy flagless ships   sound depths.

Baba Yaga

for Jane Wodening

Just get as wise as you can, the writer advises,
watching me with my son. Having raised five

children and one husband, all flown, she knows.
She lives beyond where the snowplows go,

on nuts and berries, in a crooked hut in the woods.
In winter she pulls her sled behind snowshoes,

hauling food for the duration. She leans into the wind.
You would have to know our wind. Ninety miles per hour

off the Divide, it bangs on her windows, rattles her doors.
I guess she howls at the moon, running on all fours

some nights. Her family drove her crazy, then left.
Crazy Jane, she's called. It's true her hair's a mess.

One day she will leave her cabin, and the wind
will move in. One day I will have a cabin, on a thin

trail that whispers to the ridge. I'll bury roots
in the ground, learn to bake bread in a woodstove,

stockpile cans in tiers. I'll share my berries
with the bears. I'll tame the moon, but my hair

will be a wind-torn bramble, a lightning-laced

maze. In public you won't know me. But if you brave

the weather, there will be cookies and tea. I can't
help the stories they'll tell. Just get as wise as you can.

LETHE

Between the will to do nothing and the will to do something is a thin, unchanging line: suicide.

—*Marguerite Duras*

Seroquel, quiet it, quetiapine
the line between
the will to do nothing
and the will not to do
is the river
is the Rio Grande
is the Grand, the Colorado
silted yellow

Drink, don't forget
the pills at night
quell serotonin which makes
most people happy makes most
people people
makes them alive
in love quell that
because happiness
will make you die

The line between the will
to do the will to do nothing
is a river flickering in
out of your window between
trees as you drive you
must keep to the road
you must not go down to
that yellow line

SUICIDE NOTE

And the gun whispers from
its safe   I am
here for you   I am
here   I am
safe solid easy
a little loud
that is a fact
of life   I am
a fact of life
my barrel fat
as a mother's
belly my missiles
determined as sperm   I am
oiled ready cared
for the gun calls
gently my joy
weeps gently see
how warm my handle
with its chestnut
brown wood
my steel
forged in the same
pattern for hundreds
of years   I am
tested
strong
secure
safe in your bed
under your pillow

together we can
find happiness
come bring the key
you know me
calls the gun
from behind
its lock it
softly calls how
well you know me
I am   here for you
I can make
you safe.

CAMEO

Past the gun range to the range
where the wild horses and antelope
play. The stallions are gray, dappled,
black-maned.

Mares dun, bay. A dozen or so to the
stud, mothers glad for daughters
that won't be driven away.
The plight of young males
facing battle or flight too much
for your heart, mother of sons.

And your husband says: I saw you
at the top of the ridge. Where
did you go? It's an hour later,
you've come from the road.

What brought you back
was an OHV. Is there poetry in this,
or only mystery. You went up the ridge
behind your husband, the dog,
followed no one down the trail,
suddenly faint, into an unpopulated place.

Only the tracks of unshod ponies, small
like Arabians, like the horses before
humans came. He thinks you zoned out,
walked past a whole parking lot somehow,
your own car glinting silver in the first row.

Disoriented like someone with
Alzheimer's. Is that why
the demented don't remember
the present. They are off, married to a warrior
with two toddlers. In comes a
fifty-year-old woman claiming to be a daughter.

An orange toy vehicle streaked by:
and there was the road, powerlines.
The driver, seeing something wrong,
took you back to where you
met your husband, marching.

What could you tell him?
Something glitched. There is no
explanation. Everyone is
free to form his own opinion.

BACKCOUNTRY

Corniced bowls hunched against
the west wind, the lateral snow,
the pillow of spruce below. This was
our territory. We skinned through wind-
packed drifts, limber pine krumholtz
grabbing sleeves and long hair.

I believe this land knew you. We laid
our skis on swept-bare tundra and leapt
into powder. Your son said this is what
killed you. These bowls. The Indian
Peaks. The wind and the flung snow.
Lion tracks, the trees you knew by name,

by heart: limber, whitebark, juniper,
spruce, curling in your chakras.

Niwot Ridge, where your husband
made his home, turbines spinning
to catch the power—Niwot Ridge,
sliced against the wind, is what
laid in your cancer, said your son.
Children know everything, and nothing.

Your son is dead now, suicided. Exit
bag drawn over his head. Where are
you? Do you welcome him now? In life,
this would have destroyed you. Sastrugi drifts
bury the lichens and tundra grasses

you always wanted me to be able

to name. I never did learn them,
or the names of the birds.

We were not the keen observers
we thought we were. Your husband read
your journals, named your other illness
posthumously. Your son and I resisted.
You were a poet, sensitive, visionary.
You and I, so proud of our poetic

instability. We thought the world so sick.
Our husbands so controlling. Your son
thought your husband so controlling,
the world so sick. We were daughters
of wilderness, jumpers of cornices,
fabulistas. I envied your turns,

your aura dancing in spindrift, our shadows
lost in the darker shade of the ridge.

This bowl was our secret. You wanted me
to name everything but this. I always
believed this land knew you. After
your death, your son's death, I went
to doctors of my own. We loved this wilderness,
but what drew us together was illness. I know

the name for it now. It's what the husbands
always said. My avalanche beacon pulses.

No one up here to seek it. Just me,
my dogs, and the wind. My skis whispering
after yours. Wind-hurled pellets from the far
side of the Divide bite my skin. Graupel:

You taught me that. Between snow and sleet.
It lays down fine crystals that sing.

You Can See It

for Liz

She was saying a great blue heron hurtled into her study,
    lay wing-cloaked on the plywood floor. Later, it sat up.

She was saying the elk were rearing her aborted daughter.

She was saying the mourning cloaks spattered on
    her windshield foreshadowed her death.

She was saying the passenger jets were driving the pumas
    insane.

In the end, she said, the Colorado watershed would be
    closed to humans, but one old woman would sneak
    away,

and live there.

REMANENCE

After something, someone—which is an animal?
—dies, life remains, palpable. Wakes
are held until that feeling fades. Call it

remanence, we are electromagnetic
beings, animated just as Shelley
knew, drawing lightning to us

like a sister. Remanence, place
your hands, if you are not fearful,
upon the neck. The hip,

feel molecules racing in their
confusion. Animated, specialized,
gene-coded in search of tribe.

Feel the astonishment, an entire system
atomized, each atom still alive.
Sit beside the body. It might

be frightful, because we have forgotten.
Find the tingle, the race of life
still there. It's not spooky except

if you are spooked by its enormity.
All you have to do is ask. If it
wants to find its way, it will. Whisper,

Come.

ACKNOWLEDGMENTS

Many thanks to the editors of the publications below,
in which the following poems have appeared, often in
different forms:

Adirondack Review: "Flushed"
Artful Dodge: "Trajectories," as "Traces"
Aspen Poets' Society: "After Flowers," in the anthology
    A Democracy of Poets
Awakenings Review: "Lethe," "Limbic," and "Nervestorm"
bosque magazine: [Sections of] "As the Wind Comes
    Among Us" and "Baba Yaga"
Bracken: "Backcountry" and "You Can See It"
Finishing Line Press: "Five Deer" and "Earth Shadow,"
    in the chapbook *Wild Thing in Our Known World*
Glassworks: "She who was able to embrace ..."
Green Hills Literary Lantern: "Black Bird"
Gulf Stream Magazine: "Lamictal: Prelude to the First Dose"
Literary Mama: "Fledges"
Paper Street: "Cairn Stone"
Poetry East: "Blur"
Rattle: "The Battle of Brintellix"
Sage Green Journal: "Lynx"
Spillway: "Goats" and "Headline: Mothers Given Back ..."
Tar River Poetry: "Bone Lament" and "Remanence"
Weber: The Contemporary West: "Elegy for Snow," as part
    of "Global Warming Scenarios"
The Write Launch: "Reading Octavio Paz"
The Writing Disorder: "This Isn't Really Happening"

Special thanks to ...

Everyone at Moon City Press, especially Karen Craigo & Michael Czyzniejewski; everyone at Bosque Press, especially Hilda Raz, Lynn C. Miller, & Lynda Miller; Luke Whisnant; Timothy Green; Susan Terris; Jed Myers; the Carbondale poetry group (no official name), especially Kim Nuzzo, Cameron Scott, & Marjorie DeLuca; the Aspen Poets' Society, especially Lisa Zimet (& Margie & Kim again); Bardic Trails/Talking Gourds, especially Art Goodtimes, Rosemerry Wahtola Trommer, & Daiva Chaisonis; the Aspen Writers' Network; the Glenwood Springs Writers' Group; Finishing Line Press; Community of Writers, especially Brett Hall Jones, Gregory Spatz, & Chaney Kwak; Kelli Russell Agodon; Melissa Studdard; Barbara Reese; the late Marvin Bell; Danny Rosen; Karen Glenn; Melinda Rice; Nancy Miller; Bo Cheatham; Leigh Vogel & Riccardo Savi; the Bennett Fellowship selection committee at Phillips Exeter Academy, especially Matt W. Miller, Todd Hearon, & Ralph Sneedon; Phillips Exeter in general; The Ragdale Foundation; The Kimmel Harding Nelson Center for the Arts.

And: Pamela Erens, Adrian Koesters; Kate Carroll de Gutes; Suzanne Edison, Janet and George "Van" Davis, Mary Williamson & Kurt Kiefer, Gail Mackin, Jennifer Homet Catto, Kristin Carlson, Alya Howe, Laurie Chase, Noemi Kosmowski, Dipika Rai, Marie Chan, Mical Hutson; Tory Tuttle & Paul Murphy, Cindy Foley, Sarah Ream, Erica Plouffe Lazure, Darin Pyatt, John Borstlemann, the roaming dogs of Eldora, the late Liz Caile, Jane Wodening,

Jean Kindig, Jeffrey Duvall, Kim Stefani, Debbie Cushman, Clare Shemeta, my disability lawyer Jim Cole, Judith Oakland, David Rosenthal, Peter Wiley, Majie Lavergne, Michelle Trosclair, the whole bodywork pit crew, David Weber, Margo Steeves, Kathleen Hurley.

Julian Putnam and Tony Passariello.

All my dogs, ever: Patchie, Parker, Winnipeg, Annie, Dillon, Moffat, Sally, Stephen, Sofie, Harvey, Aster, Birdie.

Cats: you know who you are.

WINNERS OF THE MOON CITY POETRY AWARD

2014
Sarah Freligh *Sad Math*

2015
Jeannine Hall Gailey *Field Guide to the End of the World*

2016
Kerri French *Every Room in the Body*

2017
Clayton Adam Clark *Finitude of Skin*

2018
Kathy Goodkin *Crybaby Bridge*

2019
Bret Shepard *Place Where Presence Was*

2020
Claudia Putnam *The Land of Stone and River*

Printed in the USA
CPSIA information can be obtained
at www.ICGtesting.com
LVHW040929070824
787563LV00004B/126